D0839293

The Give and Save 365
Easy Money Management Guide
© 2017 Laurick Ingram
All rights reserved
ISBN 13: 978-0-9991716-0-8
Library of Congress Control Number: 2017911434

THE GIVE AND SAVE

365

EASY MONEY
MANAGEMENT GUIDE

DEDICATIONS

In memory of Arimentha Ingram, my mother, who even on welfare, raising nine children, scraped together enough money to buy me books that taught me the magic of reading.

To Harold "Sonny" Ingraham, my brother from another mother. My dear, sweet, brother, I know the Alzheimer's has left me as the custodian of your memories, so although you no longer know, God knows I treasure those memories and all that you taught me.

To Kim, my wife and the mother of my children. Mom was right, you were the right one for me.

To my sons, Joshua and Jawanza, you're two of my heroes.

To my brother Ronald, for demonstrating what faith in action looks like.

To my best friend, Irving Thomas, who taught me that talent without work is like a shiny new sports car with no fuel; it may look flashy, but it is not going anywhere.

Special thanks to Armstrong Creative Consulting: Davenya, you and Sam are to Give and Save 365, what icing is to a birthday cake.

The Give and Save 365 Promise

We at Give and Save 365 promise you that with this book we will teach you a plan that, if you follow it, over time will enable you to give $10,000 to whatever church, cause, charity, group, or person you think deserves it and still have more than $30,000 left for yourself.

–Laurick Ingram
Founder / CEO
Give and Save 365, LLC

If you won't give a dime out of a dollar, you won't give $1 million out of $10 million. The time to give is now! When I had nothing, I began this process. The reward is that if you give, even at the times when you think you have very little, you'll teach your brain that there is more than enough. You can leave scarcity behind and move toward a world of abundance.

—Tony Robbins, Mastering the Money Game

CONTENTS

Preface

IV

Why I Wrote This Book

3

The 365 Easy Money Management
Five-Minute Crash Course

13

Why People Go Broke

21

How to Not Go into Debt

27

Getting Ahead and Staying Ahead

33

The Power of a Dollar a Day

39

The Give and Save 365 Promise

45

Afterword

51

PREFACE

No matter what you want out of life, four things will help you or hinder you from getting those things:

1. The *people* you know
2. The *words* you know
3. The *decisions* you make
4. The *actions* you take

Before you read another word,

ask yourself, are you

1. willing to meet new *people?*
2. willing to learn new *words?*
3. willing to make different *decisions?*
4. willing to take new *actions?*

Thank you for buying this book; my family and I appreciate it. But if your answer to the four questions above is no, you will probably not get much out of this book. You would be better off either returning it (we will give you a full refund) or giving it to a friend who is ready, willing, and open to change.

Conversely, if your answer to the four questions above is yes or even maybe, then congratulations: you have just taken the first step toward a brighter financial future.

THE GIVE AND SAVE
365
EASY MONEY
MANAGEMENT GUIDE

WHY I WROTE THIS BOOK

When I was twenty years old, working as a cashier at Quik Mart, I read a book that outlined a great strategy for saving and investing money, written by a guy who began working for $48 a week but retired with a couple million dollars in cash and assets. So, at twenty years old, I knew what to do, but I did not start doing it until twenty-five years later.

About ten years after reading that book, I met a woman named Suzy who did a lot of charitable work, including volunteering in Miami Jackson Hospital's neonatal care center. Through Suzy I met her husband, "Mo" Chorney, a silver-haired, handsome guy in his seventies who took a liking to me. Most of my life I knew a lot about working for money but knew little about getting money to work for me. For years Mo tried to teach me about managing money, and for years I did nothing with what he tried to teach me.

Then one day, it hit me. I was sitting in Mo's Florida home, in one of the two mansions he owned on Golden Beach. Mo traveled the world, made sure all his children lived in beautiful homes, and funded all his grandchildren's college educations. He owned another home in Rhode Island and several rental properties. I, on the other hand, had a great job, but if I lost that job, after six months I would have no savings left. That day I realized that one of us knew a lot about money and one of us did not. I was the one who did not.

From that day forward, I began to listen and learn from Mo. (Thank you, Mo, for being patient with me.) More importantly, I decided not only to know, but to do. I have heard the best time to plant a tree is twenty-five years ago; the second-best time is now. I could not get those twenty-five years back, so I decided to take action where I was. Eight years from that moment, my wife and I were in a position either to continue in our careers or to retire comfortably from those careers and try some new things. We both decided to try some new things, and we have never looked back nor regretted it.

The irony for us was that many of our friends—young and old—were struggling financially. These struggles seemed to cut across race, age, education, religion, and marital status. The struggles took the form of lost jobs, foreclosed homes, no money for college, repossessed cars, skyrocketing medical costs, no health insurance, or being up to their eyeballs in credit card debt.

Since my wife and I have a heart for service, we wanted to help. In many cases, we offered to meet with them, counsel them, and share how we were successful and what mistakes we had made. Maybe one out of ten of the people we talked with listened, and maybe one out of twenty-five decided to change the way they handled their money. This puzzled me because I had trouble understanding how people could spend so much time complaining or even praying about money but little or no time learning about it.

My wife suggested that I was part of the problem— that change scares a lot of people, like it did me when Mo was trying to teach me. Also, she said, the way I explained things was complex and challenged values our friends had held for most of their lives. On top of that was the fact that many people hold fast to opinions more because they are theirs than because they are right.

While I was considering my wife's observations, I attended some stewardship classes where the instructors used detailed spreadsheets to emphasize the need to budget and know where every penny goes. The presentation made sense since the people attending the classes wanted to learn about handling their money better, but I found the idea of tracking every dollar spent to be both complicated and scary, particularly because I (like most people) wasn't in the habit of doing so. This helped me see my wife's point more clearly: If it seems too complicated, most people will do nothing. If it is different from what they are used to, it scares them. I also realized that the few people we counseled who had changed their handling of money were either young adults—who were clearly open to building new habits because their other habits had not had enough time to become cast in stone; or lifetime learners who were excited about learning and trying new things.

So, back to why I wrote this book. First and foremost, I am a witness that when it comes to money, you can overcome your fears and change your habits. Next, I realized that there aren't many books on financial habits out there that are short, succinct, and easily accessible to today's busy adults. Over the years I have known many friends, associates, and coworkers who have not read a complete book since they left school. Many of these people are successful in their fields, but for whatever reason, reading an entire book is not something they enjoy or make time for. Additionally, when I first began learning how to handle money, many of the books were so thick and technical, I could not get through the first few pages before returning them to the library or putting them on my bookshelf as dust collectors. So what I did was look for books on money that children and young adults could understand. "The shorter the better" was my motto. This search inspired me to write one of my own. This book is short enough that it can be read in one sitting. (If you are one of those people who do not normally read books but are reading this one, at least if someone asks, you can answer honestly that you have read one book this year.)

Finally, I wanted to teach some financial skills in a way that was simple enough that they could be learned quickly and applied immediately (rather than waiting twenty-five years like I did). This way, my readers can start succeeding right out of the gate, because nothing feeds success like success. Now, in the words of my eleventh-grade math teacher, Lester Sandoval: "Let us move on!"

THE EASY MONEY MANAGEMENT FIVE-MINUTE CRASH COURSE

*It's not just how much you make, it's how much you keep,
and how much of what you keep makes more for you.*

-"Mo" Chorney

A few years back, my church was holding a youth conference. I was asked to speak at a breakout session designed to teach high school and college-age students about managing their money. I figured that given everything else going on at the conference, I would have the students' attention for about five minutes. My goal was to create a lesson plan that would not only teach them something about money but enable them to teach that something to someone else. This five-minute crash course is what I came up with. After I explained it to each student, he or she had to explain it back to me. Since then, I've made this my standard spiel whenever talking to young people about money for the first time.

Whenever I run into those I have taught this to, I ask them if they remember what I taught them. So far everyone has remembered. If you get nothing else out of this book, in the next five minutes you will learn something that can change the course of your financial life. Remember, first learn it, and then do it until it becomes a habit.

For as long as I can remember, my eldest brother Harold loved to quote our grandmother, Victoria McCullogh, who said, "If you make a dollar, save a dime." Years later, my pastor, Bishop Victor Curry, taught me, "If you make a dollar, tithe a dime." Because I grew to see the value in both, I taught my sons, Joshua and Jawanza: "When you get a dollar, give a dime and save a dime." If you develop that habit, for every dollar you get, you will know you are enriching your own life as well as the lives of others.

The Five-Minute Crash Course

When it comes to your money, you are doing one of three Gs with it. You are

1. going broke;

2. going into debt; or

3. getting ahead.

The good news is, if you are not doing the third G, you can start getting ahead today. The table on the next page shows you how. Go to our website (www.giveandsave365. com), download it, and then sign it, date it, and put in somewhere you will see it several times a day. It will show you how to get to and stay in the third G method of managing your money.

THE EASY MONEY MANAGEMENT FIVE-MINUTE CRASH COURSE

1. GOING BROKE HABIT OF MONEY MANAGEMENT

YOU MAKE, GET AN ALLOWANCE, OR GIFT OF	$100
YOU SPEND ON BILLS OR PURCHASES	-$100
YOU HAVE LEFT UNTIL YOU GET MORE	$0

2. GOING INTO DEBT HABIT OF MONEY MANAGEMENT

YOU MAKE, GET AN ALLOWANCE, OR GIFT OF	$100
YOU SPENT ON BILLS OR PURCHASES	-$100
YOU BORROWED	-$10
THE NEXT $100 YOU GET YOU ALREADY OWE	-$10

3. GETTING AND STAYING AHEAD HABIT OF MONEY MANAGEMENT

YOU MAKE, GET AN ALLOWANCE, OR GIFT OF	$100
YOU SPENT ON BILLS OR PURCHASES	-$80
YOU SAVED (YOU PAID YOURSELF FIRST)	$10
YOU GAVE (YOU HELPED SOMEBODY)	$10
YOU HAVE LEFT UNTIL YOU GET MORE	+$10

I WILL REMEMBER, WHEN I MAKE A DOLLAR, TO GIVE A DIME AND SAVE A DIME, BECAUSE WHEN IT COMES TO MONEY, IT IS NOT ONLY HOW MUCH I MAKE, BUT HOW MUCH I KEEP AND HOW MUCH OF WHAT I KEEP, KEEPS WORKING FOR ME INSTEAD OF ME WORKING FOR IT.

NAME: _____ DATE: _____

We guarantee you will feel good about what you are doing with your money and what your money is doing for you and others.

By signing, dating and putting it where you will see it every day, you are planting it in your mind, where it can take root and grow and blossom into a habit for life. That ends your five-minute crash course on money management. If you want to learn more, read on, but if you learn and do this one thing, it will change your ideas about money forever. When it comes to your dollars, your new habit, starting today, is to always be *getting and staying ahead.*

WHY PEOPLE GO BROKE

Knowing "ain't" doing!

-Laurick Ingram

If a person loses his or her job or has no money coming in to start with, in that case the person needs to get a job, sell something, provide a service, or get an allowance, but he or she somehow must get some money coming in. Believe it or not, that is not the problem I see the most. Most of the people I know who out of their own mouths say they are "broke" are receiving money from some source on a regular basis. If you ask many of them whether they are taking in more money now than they were ten years ago, their answer will usually be yes, yet they are just as broke as they were or have more debt than they did ten years ago.

If you are in the habit of being broke, after reading this book you will know how to change that. But be warned: knowing what to do is easier than doing it. Knowing you need to study for a test is easier than turning off the computer or putting down the cell phone and studying. Knowing you could stand to lose a few pounds is a lot easier than not eating those triple chocolate chunk cookies (I kid you not, those rascals call out to me late at night). Knowing you should give and save money instead of spending it is a lot easier than giving and saving those dollars.

How, then, do you make doing these things easy? By deciding to do them and then repeating the action enough until doing it becomes automatic. For example, most people decided a long time ago which hand they would hold their forks in. When they sit down to eat, they don't labor over which hand to use; they grab the fork with the same hand they have used for years and start eating. The reason many people stay broke is they decided a long time ago that they would spend money as fast as they got it. Then they kept doing it until it became as much a habit as how they held their forks.

The goal is to get to where giving and saving 10 percent of all you get becomes automatic. But for many people, this terrifies them. It scares them so much that they end up doing nothing. My goal is for you to start giving and saving today for the next 365 days until it becomes a lifetime habit where, whenever you make a dollar, you automatically give a dime and save a dime.

HOW TO NOT GO INTO DEBT

Everything should be as simple as it can be,
but not simpler.

—Albert Einstein (Attributed)

I will make this as simple as possible. The way to not go into debt is to not go into debt—and if you are already in debt, to not go deeper in debt. If you already owe a family member $20, don't borrow another $20 from a friend or other family member until you pay back the first $20 you borrowed. (Yes, you should pay your family or friends back if you borrowed money from them, and they shouldn't have to remind you.) Few people can afford to buy a car or house using cash; therefore, you will probably have to finance these two big ticket items. As far as everything else goes, pay cash, or if you charge it, pay off your credit card at the end of each month. If you already have balances on your charge card(s), do not charge anything else until you have paid them off.

But you say, "I can't start saving until I am out of debt." Wrong! You just have to treat your dollar a little differently from people who don't have debt. You must give a dime, save a dime, and pay two dimes toward what you owe. You must save, because if you do not save, the first time you need money for something important, you will have to borrow it, and voilà—I have always liked that word—more debt. Also, for every dollar you save, your debt is decreased. For example, if you owe $10 and have $0 saved, your net worth (what you have minus what you owe) is -$10. If you owe $10 but have $1 saved, your net worth is $9, 10 percent more than before. If you keep saving and growing your money, your net worth will overtake your debt, but more importantly, you will have developed the habit of getting ahead and staying ahead (which I'll discuss in the next chapter).

GETTING AHEAD AND STAYING AHEAD

When presenting new ideas, tell your audience what you are going to tell them, tell them, then tell them what you told them.

-Ms. Yvonne Gable, My High School English Teacher

Getting ahead is a direction, not a destination. The best way to keep going broke or get into more debt is to repeat the habits that got you there and keep you there. The way to get ahead is to decide you want to get ahead and then build the habits that drive you in that direction.

At the beginning of this book, I wrote the following:

Before you read another word,

ask yourself, are you

1. willing to meet new *people?*
2. willing to learn new *words?*
3. willing to make different *decisions?*
4. willing to take new *actions?*

To go ahead, get ahead, and stay ahead, your lifetime assignment starting today will be to meet people who use the words, make the decisions, and take the actions that drive them in that direction—people whose conversations include statements like these:

- **I paid my sister back** the money I borrowed from her without her having to ask me for it. Yes, you should pay family and friends back money that you borrowed without them having to be reminded by you.

- **I paid cash for the new shoes I bought for** the party next week.

- All my credit **cards** are **paid off,** and if I use one, **I pay it off by the end of the month.**

- I am going **to wait** until I can pay cash for a new television before I get it.

- Every two **weeks, I put money away** for Christmas (or whatever holiday you celebrate) so that I do not have to charge any gifts.

- I **volunteer** for something or someone I care about.

- I have **an automatic deduction plan** that puts money into my retirement account.

- I have an **automatic savings account** for vacations and emergencies.

- Or my personal favorite, I **give and save 365** days a year, but you say, "I don't get money everyday." I understand that, maybe you get money once a week, once a month or once in while. The point is that everyday, you can decide when you get it, to give and save some of it. This way no matter when it comes you are ready.

This book is meant to offer ideas that you can choose to sow into your thoughts until they take hold and grow into action. Emerson said: "Sow a thought and you reap an act; sow an act and you reap a habit; sow a habit and you reap a character; sow a character and you reap a destiny." A bright and great financial destiny awaits you.

THE POWER OF A DOLLAR A DAY

*Small things done are worth more
than great things planned.*

—Something I Saw on a Secretary's Bulletin Board

A long time ago, King Solomon wrote, "Start children off on the way they should go, and even when they are old they will not turn from it." Many of our money troubles grow out of bad habits we begin when we are young, and they keep repeating until they become like old friends. One aim of this book is to help you start giving and saving as soon as you can in your life—and the sooner, the better.

Robert G. Allen said, "One dollar a day can make you a millionaire or it can bankrupt you. A dollar a day flowing into your life from interest can make you a fortune or it can bankrupt you by flowing out of your life." Here is the proof.

First, if you earned $1 a day for a year, at the end of the year you would have $365. If you spent it all, in forty years you would have nothing—unless what you spent it on lasted forty years, which is unlikely.

Second, if you borrowed a $1 a day for one year only, at the end of the year you would have borrowed $365. Let's say you don't have to make any payments for forty years, but the interest rate is 20 percent (the amount some credit card companies charge). In forty years, you would owe a little over a million dollars.

But if you saved $1 a day for one year, at the end of the year you would have $365. If you earned 20 percent on that money over the next forty years, you would have $1,018,623.

That is why a dollar a day flowing into your life can make you a fortune, whereas $1 a day flowing out of your life can bankrupt you. Make sure the dollars are flowing into your life and the lives of others.

THE GIVE AND SAVE 365 PROMISE

The best way to learn something is to teach it.

—Stephen Covey, quoting his professor, Dr. Walter A. Gong

At the beginning of the book I promised you that I would teach you a plan that would allow you over time to give away $10,000 and, after doing so, still have more than $30,000 left for yourself.

An Easy 365 Plan to Build Savings

If you commit to giving a $1 a day ($30.42 a month) to whatever church, cause, charity, group, or person you consider worthy and at the same time put $1 a day ($30.42 a month) in an investment account earning a 7.2 percent return, at the end of twenty-eight years you will have given away $10,220, but in your account, you will have $32,768. There is your plan to give away $10,000 and end up with three times what you gave away.

That's the plan; check the math.

***

The small lessons you've learned in this book, if you practice them, are worth far more than the big ideas you never get around to doing. Said another way, a dollar a day saved and invested over time is worth more than the hundreds or thousands you plan to save but never get around to actually saving.

AFTERWORD

Give and Save 365, LLC, was founded by my wife and me. The company's mission is: "Teaching you how to use every dollar you get to add value to your life and the lives of others." I agree with Stephen Covey, that teaching something requires a deeper understanding than just learning it. I am encouraging you not only to develop your own lifetime habit of giving and saving, but to teach at least one other person what you have learned. All you need is a willing heart and $2.

I close with the parable of the ten birds. If ten birds are sitting on a fence, and one decides to fly away, how many birds are left on the fence? Ten birds are left, because deciding to fly is not the same as flapping your wings and taking off.

I say to you, do not learn this today and then wait twenty-five years to start doing it. Right here, right now, take off!

Thank you for sharing your

precious time with us.

God bless!

Laurick Ingram